An Hour to Live,
an Hour to Love

An Hour to Live, an Hour to Love

THE TRUE STORY
OF THE BEST GIFT
EVER GIVEN

Richard Carlson, Ph.D.,
and Kristine Carlson

 NEW YORK

Library of Congress Cataloging-in-Publication Data

Carlson, Richard.
    An hour to live, an hour to love : the true story of the best gift ever given / Richard Carlson and Kristine Carlson.—1st ed.
      p.   cm.
    ISBN-13: 978-1-4013-2257-1
    ISBN-10: 1-4013-2257-3
    1. Love. 2. Man-woman relationships. 3. Friendship. 4. Bereavement.
5. Husbands—Death—Psychological aspects. I. Carlson, Kristine. II. Title.
    BF575.L8C244   2007
    158—dc22   2007013282

Hyperion books are available for special promotions and premiums. For details contact Michael Rentas, Proprietary Markets, Hyperion, 77 West 66th Street, 12th floor, New York, New York 10023, or call 212-456-0133.

Design by Victoria Hartman

FIRST EDITION

10 9 8 7 6 5 4 3 2 1

I dedicate this book in loving memory

to my husband,

soul mate, and best friend,

Richard Carlson

A gentle man who walked the earth

in peace and loving kindness,

teaching the world how to be happy—

no matter what.

Contents

Acknowledgments

FIRST AND FOREMOST I would like to thank the millions of people around the world who have read and loved Richard's books and sent their condolences and prayers. We have been comforted and felt the strength of your support.

I would like to acknowledge the following people who helped me to publish this book at a truly difficult time in my life: Patti Breitman, who came out of retirement to represent and support me and pay tribute to Richard's legacy and life through this book; our foreign rights agent, Linda Michaels, for her loving friendship and encouragement; Natalie Tucker for her coaching/editing to help me stay focused during some of my lowest times in this grieving process; Leslie Wells and Bob Miller for their faith in this book. A special thanks to all the earthly angels, our friends and family, who stepped forward to light our path through the valley of darkness of grief.

Mostly, I'd like to thank my daughters, Jasmine and Kenna. You have taken care of me as much as I have you these past months. You are the reason I would die and you became my reason to live. Your daddy is so proud of you and you know how much he loves you! Though this is one of the most difficult time periods you'll ever endure, I am so proud of how you show up in life every day and what amazing young ladies you are. The four of us will always be united by one great love—family.

Introduction

MY HUSBAND HELD my hand and led me down a footpath, carrying a bundle tied with a gold ribbon, to our favorite bench hidden within a private canopy of cypress and pine that overlooked the Pacific Ocean. It was about twenty minutes before sunset and as we sat, my face snuggled into his shoulder, our arms wrapped around each other, we savored the moment, grateful to be viewing another one of nature's treasures. He silently handed me the packet sitting on his lap. The letters jumped off the cover sheet, which read:

An Hour to Live:

Who would you call, and why are you waiting?

To Kris, the love of my life,

on our eighteenth wedding anniversary.

Love, Richard

It was an awkward moment for me as I presented him with only a card.

Sitting on the cliff while Richard watched the sun receding, I read the most beautiful piece of writing I could ever imagine. Even from Richard Carlson, the prolific author, this was an astounding gift to receive. I wondered, Where did this come from?

As I turned to face him, tears streaming down my face, I asked him if he was terminally ill. He laughed and replied, "No, not ill. I am inspired by our love and the beauty of life. I had to say these things."

How poignant and powerful his message is now. Three years later, during the most sorrow-filled moments of my life, as I grieve his premature death and the loss of my true love and the plans that we had for our future together that will never happen, I remember his letter to me—the best gift ever given. All the Tiffany pouches and other beautiful things that money can buy pale in comparison to the evident love that leaps from these pages. There is one thing that I know with every breath and every fiber of my being, and it is that love is truly eternal and lasts forever. It is the core of our connection and expression of life; it is where Richard will remain pure and alive. I am united with him for all time. This gift holds the power of hope and comfort for me and our daughters as we grieve his loss and step into a new life. In considering his mortality, it is as if Richard knew deep in his unconscious that there was the possibility, as there is for any of us, that he might depart suddenly. In sharing his heartfelt love and appreciation, he gave an example to all of us of how completely and fully we can live. He gave me something of him that will help to sustain me for the rest of my life.

I will hold Richard in my heart forever, knowing that he loved me fully and held precious all that we shared and all that we created in our twenty-five years together. I have few regrets as I remember with delight and heartfelt appreciation all of the magical moments. I hope that you pass this on to someone special and remember what Richard said often: "You will be remembered most, not from your accomplishments in life, but for how well you lived and how much love you carried in your heart."

Treasure the gift of life, and enjoy this true story of the best gift ever given.

An Hour to Live,
an Hour to Love

An Hour to Live

by Richard Carlson

I'VE ALWAYS BELIEVED that when reflecting on a life worth living, in which you are going to cherish every step along the way, it's a good idea to jump ahead and look back. This is a great way to get immediate and accurate perspective about what's really important right now.

My absolute favorite quotation is from author Stephen Levine. He says, "If you had an hour to live and could make just one phone call, who would it be to, what would you say...and why are you waiting?" None of us knows, of course, how long we have to live. Even fewer of us realize what a blessing in disguise this "curse" of knowing we will one day die really is. It encourages us to live on the edge, not to take life for granted, and to be grateful for what we have, treating life as the miracle it truly is.

My first, forced exposure to this wisdom occurred eighteen years ago when one of my best friends, Robert, and his dear friend were killed by a drunk driver on their way to my wedding in Oregon. Robert was to be in our wedding party two days later, as one of my groomsmen. His death woke me up and slowed me down. It was the saddest moment of my life, and it shook me to my core.

I've met hospice workers whom I consider to be

saints. Many have said to me, half kidding of course, "I keep waiting for one person to look back on his life and say to me, 'I wish I had been more uptight.'" If we all take even a moment to think about it, we know in our hearts that when we look back on our own lives, we won't wish we had worried more about the small stuff!

Since we know we are going to die someday, and that we are going to look back on our lives and reflect on what's important, why not start living that way today? Right now? Why not plan our lives, our jobs, our day-to-day, moment-to-moment experiences based on the inevitable moment of reflection that will be upon us sooner than any of us can possibly imagine? It's no coincidence that one of the most widely used phrases is "time flies." It really does.

Even so, if we could only live the way we know deep down we should, we would guarantee ourselves a life of richness and fulfillment. If we answer Stephen Levine's question honestly and act accordingly, we will have no regrets—none whatsoever.

Who Would You Call?

If I had an hour to live, I'll tell you who I wouldn't call. It wouldn't be my stockbroker, my financial planner, my banker, or my CPA. Don't get me wrong. They're all great people, but the last thing on my mind would be how much money I had made during my lifetime or, for that matter, how much I had left. Things that once seemed important, like the rate of return on my investment portfolio or my current tax bracket, would seem entirely irrelevant. We spend so much of our lives collecting achievements and then identifying ourselves with them. Yet, with an hour to live, those achievements don't seem very relevant. I wouldn't be looking at my trophies.

Likewise, I wouldn't be checking in at the office to see what last-minute projects I might be able to check off my list! After all, my in box is always full. I wouldn't be checking my voice mail, my pager, my e-mail, or my Palm Pilot. All the so-called emergencies would have to wait. I always wondered if the world would come to an end if I didn't get to all these things. Imagining myself looking around, about ready to leave this place, I finally have my answer. The world looks as crazy as ever, but it's clearly going to go on without me. I guess I was mistaken about the relative importance of my little corner. I think I may have taken myself a bit too seriously.

If I had an hour to live, I also wouldn't be calling anyone who owed me any money, or anyone who had wronged me in any way during my lifetime. I wonder how much time I fretted away, over the years, thinking about that kind of stuff. It's not worth one second's thought. With the time I have left, I choose to allow my thoughts to rest in total peace, right here, right now in this precious moment.

If I wanted to, I could convince myself that lots of people owe me favors, but, do you know what? This isn't the time to think about it. I guess life isn't about keeping track after all. As it turns out, it's easier and a lot more fun to simply give things away and be happy about it. In the end, it takes far less energy to give than it does to receive, and what's more, giving provides its own source of joy. When you give something away, whether it's your love, compassion, an idea, your energy, an insight, some money, a possession, creativity, passion, time, some kindness, or whatever else you have to offer, it feels really good and, in the end, that's what it's all about. I've never regretted an act of kindness, and I've never met a single person in my entire life who said to me, "I wish I had been less kind or less generous."

Like a lot of people over the age of forty, I've struggled a little bit with my weight in recent years. I can tell you with absolute certainty, however, that I wouldn't be calling a dietitian or my physician, or watching a last-minute infomercial, hoping for a miracle diet pill that was going to make me look ten years younger and fifteen pounds lighter. Nope, I'm certain that any extra weight I'm carrying would be about as important as the size of my bank account. On a scale of one to ten, it would be a zero.

And another thing. If I had an hour to live, I wouldn't be calling the lawyer who will be handling all my "stuff" after I'm gone. I never really did care for all this stuff anyway. It always seemed like a burden to me, as if I were tripping over it all. There always seemed to be too much of it to deal with. I had to buy it, clean it, store it, keep it, insure it, keep track of it, find places for it, move it around, replace and update it, and now, in the end, decide who gets it next. Who cares?

No, if had an hour to live and I could make only one call, it would be to my life partner, Kris. The two of us have been married for eighteen years, but far more important than that, to me, is the fact that we've been best friends for more than twenty years. It's hard to write this without tears coming to my eyes because I know, someday, I will have to make this call. And when I do, I hope I'll be able to call Kris. Better yet, I hope I'll be able to be with her.

There's no single way to describe the best thing about our partnership. Part of it is the laughter. There has been so much laughing. When we're together, life seems so funny so much of the time. I don't always know whether she's laughing at me or with me, but whichever it is, she helps me to not take myself, or life, very seriously. I've never known anyone as completely humble as Kris. She's just herself, and she's completely comfortable with who she is.

When we first met, I was a top-ranked competitive college tennis player with plans to turn professional. The problem was, my heart wasn't in it anymore. But I was a real people pleaser who had a difficult time listening to my own heart and letting people down. I felt trapped. Virtually everyone I knew encouraged me to keep playing. "After all," they would say, "you've got a lot of potential. You're a good college player, and you might even make it big as a pro." Who cared if I was miserable?

But it turned out someone did care, and that someone was Kris. She was the first person I met who said to me, "Richard, if you're not happy, it's time to quit being competitive and start listening to your heart. It's time to change direction." A month later, I was spending time as a Big Brother for the Big Brothers of America program, phasing out of competitive tennis. It was one of the first times I had listened to my heart instead of my head. As a Big Brother, I was focusing on someone else's needs instead of my own, so it was also one of the first times I felt the intense inner joy and satisfaction of giving. Those few hours a week meant more to me than the rest of the week combined, and I did not miss tennis one bit. That was a major turning point in my life, and I owe it to Kris.

Kris and I both agree that our greatest joy has been sharing our life with our two children, Jazzy and Kenna. Like many parents, I can't begin to explain the joy they have brought to our lives. I wouldn't have traded my time with them for the world. Their personalities are unique, and underscore the fact that we can't take any credit for who they are. We cared for them and guided them the best we could, and even though we got in the way every once in a while, I have a feeling they are going to turn out pretty darned well.

God was kind enough to share Jazzy and Kenna with us, and that's always what it has seemed like to us, a blessing and a privilege. They are both headed their own ways now, and the gratitude I feel that I've been able to be here to watch them grow up and be a part of their lives is beyond words. I don't regret a millisecond of my time with them. Now I can actually say with some authority that it's true; it's really true. You won't regret saying no to the office and to your boss and to other obligations in order to say yes to your children and to your partner and to your family. I know it can seem hard to do sometimes, but do you know what? When it's your turn to look back someday, you're going to be glad you did, I'm 100 percent certain. So don't feel guilty. Just make the right choices. In the end, you'll be so glad you did. I guarantee it.

What Would You Say?

In the last hour of my life, I hope I would already have said my good-byes to all my friends, family, and my two daughters. With one hour to live and only one person to share it with, I would choose to be at home with my wife, Kris, preferably beside a crackling fire, rain dancing on the roof above us. And what would I say to her? I think, if I could, I would say something like this . . .

"Kris, mostly I want to tell you how much I love and cherish you, and how much I cherish our relationship. There are just a few things I want you to know before I say good-bye.

"To begin, I want you to know that if I could live this life again with you, I'd do so in a heartbeat. Thank you for being there for me so many times when I proved to be oh-so-human. Thank you for accepting me, flaws and all, for taking my hand in yours, and for loving me during my highest highs and my lowest lows. You always encouraged me to follow my heart and when I forgot to listen, you'd sit quietly with me and place my hand on my heart to help remind me. You always told me that following my heart was far more important than any amount of success, and that what you wanted most was for me to be happy. And I always knew that you were telling me the truth.

"Thank you for being such a great mother to our beautiful girls. I never told you enough how much I appreciated the daily love you showered on our family and the incredible kindness you shared with so many people in our community, and beyond. I feel so lucky to have shared my life with someone who is so kind, every single day.

"What I remember most dearly are the times we walked hand in hand with the kids by the ocean. How I always loved the sound of the waves crashing, the beautiful rocks, the birds flying overhead, and the occasional whale swimming by. I loved how the wind would take your hair and randomly mess it up—and I loved even more that you never cared.

"I have loved, too, the walks we took in our garden in the summers and, especially, looking at the sunflowers you planted every year. Your favorite flower—always smiling, beautiful, open, and friendly! Remember how we always said it's hard to be depressed when you see a sunflower, how we picked them together when they were ready and brought them inside to brighten our home?

"Times weren't always happy or easy. But as I look back, even the periods that seemed so difficult at the time, now appear to me as necessary parts of the journey, integral pieces of the tapestry of our lives together.

"You probably remember all too well that pivotal time in my writing career when I almost couldn't take it anymore and was considering giving up. Writing was my passion, my dream job, which I loved even when doing it for free. The problem was, even after nine books and two children, that's pretty much all I was doing! We were making hardly any money from the books, and I had to work on them in the middle of the night because I was doing other things during the day to pay the bills.

"I remember fantasizing about how great it would be not to need any sleep and actually bragging to you and others about getting less than four hours' rest each night. You said to me, 'Be careful what you ask for,' and, boy, were you right. Little did I know that my obsession would become a major sleep disorder, insomnia and all. It's funny. I spent the first twelve years of our marriage trying to stay awake, and every night since then desperately trying to get some sleep!

"When we had finally made some money, I decided to start my own Internet company. Clearly, I had lost my humility, and I guess I thought I had the magic touch. Well, that didn't last very long, did it? I love the way you kept your sense of humor during that ordeal. I must have seemed like such an idiot, but you just thought the whole thing was incredibly funny. Even when I told you I thought we could lose everything and you saw the fear in my eyes, all you did was listen. You never lost your cool or gave me any harsh lectures.

"Instead, Kris, you kept insisting that we had

each other, that the kids were healthy, and that this was all that was ultimately important. Now, with that chaos and nonsense behind me, I can see that you were right. Even if we had lost it all, it would not have been the end of the world. We would have found a way to get by, just like everyone else. I learned so much about greed through that experience and about how seductive it is. I've seen how much nicer our lives have been since, and how much more content we've been with what we have.

"How many times have we lain in bed drinking coffee together, early in the morning? It must be thousands. That has always been my favorite ritual with you—coffee first, then our short meditation. Isn't it funny that everything we loved together never cost much money? I remember when we were really young and you gave me that sign that said THE BEST THINGS IN LIFE AREN'T THINGS. You sure were right about that. You know, Kris, you were right about a lot of things. I got a lot of public credit as the years went along, but you were actually the one who was so on-target.

"Do you remember the night my grandma Emily died? I had spent so much time with her in her final days, but I wasn't able to be with her when she passed away. When my dad called me to let me know, I couldn't quite keep it together. When I hung up the phone, I put my head down on the table and started to cry. You came into the room and knew immediately what had happened—you knew she was gone. What I remember is that you held me for a long, long time. After what must have been an hour or more you said, 'Grandma is perfectly fine now, and she still loves you so very much. It's going to be OK.' Kris, I don't know if it was what you said or how you said it, but that really helped.

"Big stuff aside, in our life together there have been times—hundreds of them—when I sweated something small. You always simply smiled and said, 'Well, we always teach best what we most need to learn,' reminding me gently that I am not exempt from the problems of humanity.

"If I could live this life over again, I'd spend less time talking and more time listening, particularly to you and to the children. Saying good-bye to the girls, I cried when I realized I hadn't listened nearly enough to them over the years, and they have so much to say. In my attempts to share my own wisdom, I have missed out on hearing theirs. That's something I'd change for sure, and it would have been easy to do.

"Remember when Jazzy and I went to the coast for a father-daughter date? She was about five years old. She spent an hour in the hotel room getting all dressed up in her most beautiful outfit and, after telling her how beautiful she was, I said I would love to take her anywhere she would like for dinner—somewhere down by the water. She thought about it for a minute and she had her answer: 'Taco Bell!' So Taco Bell it was, in her lovely dress, sitting on the cliff, looking out at the Pacific Ocean. She still remembers that 'date,' and so do I.

"When Kenna was six, she and I went up to the mountains and stayed in a nice resort hotel near

Lake Tahoe. Our plan was to play in the snow that day, but we were having so much fun in the room, we never made it outside. Kenna jumped from bed to bed and drew pictures she stuck all over the windows with tape. We played games that she made up as she went along, and the room service was just perfect! It was after midnight when she finally fell asleep in my arms. I felt so young that day. I'll never forget just holding her and looking at her, with happy tears in my eyes, wondering to myself, how in the world I ever ended up so lucky.

"If I could live my life over again, Kris, I'd spend far less energy wanting things I didn't have, and far more energy enjoying what I already did have. It's such an obvious thing, and it's right under our noses our entire lifetime—the idea that happiness comes not from getting what we want, but instead from wanting what we have. You always seemed to know this.

"Another thing I'm absolutely certain of is this: If I could live my life over again, I'd rarely if ever be in such a hurry. What is the point? You get to the end of your life and you finally pause and reflect, and it all becomes so clear. You see the absurdity of all the rushing around. In fact, it looks so funny and ridiculous. The 'rat race' is an illusion, and so unnecessary. We rush around, and for what? All it does is keep us from truly experiencing life in any sort of meaningful, deep way. I can now see that people are trying to chase happiness. It's ironic, however, because if we would just slow down, happiness would catch up to us.

"I spent half my life trying to teach others to be

'present' but, looking back, my own hurrying kept me from being as present as I might have been. I could have been even happier and more joyful than I was by simply slowing down and enjoying the trip. Where was I running to anyway? I was always right here, and I'm still right here! It all seems so funny now, and so obvious.

"That's one of the things I admire the most about you, Kris—your ability to be present with me, and with others, and with life in general. You don't rush around as much as most of us do. You seem to be able to 'be here now' whenever you're with me. That's why I have always felt so special around you. When I'm with you, I sense that there's no place you'd rather be, even when I know you have a ton of things you need to get done. I never felt like we had to rush off to Paris or Rome to have fun. It was always fun to just sit and be with you. It always felt like a vacation when you'd take my hand after a long day and we'd walk together into the backyard. And then we'd just sit down and have a cold drink of water. Remember how I used to joke with you that a half hour with you in the backyard was more relaxing than three days at an expensive spa? You knew just what I needed and how to slow me down just by being calm yourself. What a gift that was to me, all these years.

"If I could live my life over again, I would never put off so easily and so often, what I knew, deep down, I really wanted to do. God, if I had only known what a mistake that was. I mean I thought I knew, I really did, but I still did it—I put off the really important stuff. I'd say things like, 'This is a really busy time,' as if, somehow, next month was magically going to be less demanding. I fell for my own rap, the very things I was teaching others not to do. You always had the attitude that there is no time like the present to go have some fun—and that the piles of paper and the unreturned phone calls will still be there when we get back. And you were always right. So you'd take my hand and gently squeeze it, and off we'd go. Thank God one of us had some common sense!

"What I've loved most about you, Kris, is that I never, even once since I've known you, felt that you didn't love or accept me exactly as I am. When I was on top of the world, it didn't impress you very much, and when I was down and out, you were always there for me, every single time. Nothing fazed you, and you never expected me to be perfect, to be anything but an ordinary guy with flaws and struggles just like everyone else. Even when the world around me assumed that everything was OK but deep inside I was suffering, you didn't even flinch; you simply kept on loving me. You loved me as unconditionally as anyone really can, just as I've seen you do for others—your friends, our kids, other family members, and people we were trying to help. To be loved in that way, by the very person you love more than anyone else in this world, that's a really incredible feeling. I don't even know what to say about that except, if I could live this life again, I'd like to be more that way myself.

"It's been said that as you look back on your life, it flashes before your eyes. That's not quite what I'm experiencing, but a few things are becoming crystal clear. If I could live my life over, I'd be more loving to you and to everyone else as well—and I'd expect far less in return. I see now that life is all about love, sharing, compassion, and kindness. Mother Teresa said, 'We cannot do great things on this earth. We can only do small things with great love.' I'm so glad we have lived our lives sharing this principle, knowing, too, that even small things can be great things when our hearts are in the right place.

"I'm so proud of you, Kris, and so grateful that you're one of the people in this world whose heart is in the right place. You must have asked me a hundred times, 'Why are we here, anyway?' And, by your side, I've come to believe that the answer to that question is that we are here to serve others, and to serve God. Everything else is secondary, because love, kindness, compassion, closeness, and a generous spirit last forever.

"I'll never forget you, Kris, and I'll never forget our two magnificent children. Thank you for sharing your life with me. Everything is going to be fine now. I know it is for me, and especially for you and for the girls. You all have so much wisdom and so much to look forward to. I love you all so much. This has been a magnificent journey.

"It's almost time for me to say good-bye, and I know in my heart it's not going to be for good. I know I'll see you again—somehow, some way, somewhere, in some form. I'd like to spend the moments we have left just being quiet with you, listening to the rain and the crackle of the fire. I want to hug you one last time—a big bear hug. If I could live this life again, I'd spend a lot more time hugging people, especially you and our girls. Thank you, Kris. Thanks for just being you. I love you."

Why Are You Waiting?

The key to a good life is this: If you're not going to talk about something during the last hour of your life, then don't make it a top priority during your lifetime.

When you really think about it, it's a miracle that we're even here to begin with. Life itself is such an awesome adventure! When Kenna was very young, she used to wake up in the morning and say to Kris, "Mommy, I get another one of these?" meaning, "I get another day!" I got goose bumps whenever I heard her say it. She was hitting the nail squarely on the head. Imagine being so full of gratitude that you wake up every day happy just to be alive, breathing the air, enjoying the beauty of the natural world, and maybe even sitting next to someone you love. In a nutshell, that's what's valuable about knowing we're about to die. All of a sudden, the moment we're in, this one right now, fills us with positive thoughts and feelings. If we could all only realize what a miracle life is, our lives would mean much more to us on a day-to-day, moment-to-moment basis.

Don't misunderstand what I'm saying. We all have obligations, responsibilities, goals, and priorities that are relevant, such as our financial security, career status, and social prestige. We have goals, dreams, ambitions, and obstacles to overcome. We also have unique challenges to face, hurdles to climb, people to meet, all sorts of relationships to foster, and on and on. We even have superficial stuff on our agendas such as our lifestyle, how much money we make, the kind of car we drive, the possessions we accumulate, how we look, and so forth. All of this is fine and good and reasonable. But none of it is what's going to make us happy.

What is going to make us happy and content is that "critical inch," the stuff we will talk about in that final hour of our life. We need to make choices in our lives right now based on what's truly important. So, who would you speak to if you had only an hour to live? What would you talk about in that final hour? Most importantly, why are you waiting?

An Hour to Love

by Kristine Carlson

I WRITE THIS as a tribute to the authenticity of Richard's wisdom. As his wife, I can testify to how he lived and what he did best: love fully and live presently. I write this as an extension of his message, and as a way to give back to all those who gave so much to us over the years. I write this as a response to his gift to me, three years prior to his death, on our eighteenth wedding anniversary. I also write this as a gift to myself and our daughters, Jasmine and Kenna, in the beginning of this incredibly full process of grieving his loss.

This response seems to come from an ending, or at least that is what others would have you believe, judging from the sentiments expressed in their sympathy cards. Richard's death has rocked me to my core, cracking wide open the deepest parts of me, leaving me as vulnerable and exposed as I have ever been. In this opening, to my surprise, I have discovered a miracle.

In Richard's death, I have awoken from a deep slumber to the rebirth of my spirit. This process (and it is a process) has been both excruciating and at times, actually, blissful. "Bliss" is not a word generally associated with death, in the minds of anyone I know, including myself. Yet, this is what I have discovered.

In life, Richard and I shared a remarkable connection, one that does not die with the body. The first time we met, it was like coming home. Our love grew, and we grew together as soul mates and partners in every sense of the word. Our life together spanned twenty-five years, and there was never a doubt that we would be together for the whole of our lifetimes, which we believed would be much longer.

Then, on December 13, 2006, Richard walked out the door, caught a flight, and didn't come back. He died a sudden and painless death from a pulmonary embolism, while asleep.

I now understand, why when one partner passes, after being together for many years, the other often leaves shortly after. I am just forty-three, and know how unbearably painful the longing of separation feels; the emptiness, at times, brings me to my knees. If I did not continue to feel Richard's love and to connect with him, deep in my spirit, I would not survive this loss. Of that I am 100 percent certain.

Grieving is the ultimate act of love, or, at least, it can be. Love holds all possibilities, and that includes bliss in the face of immeasurable suffering and gain through loss. I am relieved that in this process there are these small treasures, because I don't think anyone would emerge from this kind of grief if there weren't.

Because of love, there is a beginning in this end. Because of the enormous love Richard and I shared over our years together, I am capable of so much more than falling into the abyss of sorrow in his absence. One thing I am completely aware of is that

I am faced with a choice in how I decide to live on in this journey. It is as if I am facing two doors. As I turn right, I open the door to breathtaking light, divine consciousness, and abundant love. As I turn left, I open the door to the complete and utter darkness of the blackest night. As I stand facing both doors, embracing both possibilities, I realize the power of my choices.

Life is a series of choices potentially taking us to many places, and even as you think prior to tragedy that you could not possibly survive, there is still a choice in how you go on. I never dreamed I would be able to live one hour without Richard, and truthfully after an initial death wish upon learning that that hour was now, the image of my daughters came to me, and I knew I had to and I would go on. Choosing to leave was simply not an option. In what ways are we not always choosing and manifesting our own destiny, constantly choosing which door to open?

On different days, as I fully experience the humanness of my grief, I will choose a different door and move through each moment as it presents itself, embracing both the dark and the light, living the fullness of this curriculum. The truth is, amidst the regret, longing, and bereavement I also experience enormous gratitude for the opening and awakening of this experience, as I vow to never sleepwalk through life again. When it is said life goes on for the living, we should correct this statement by saying life goes on for the living who are fully awake.

Often when people express their sympathies,

they say how sorry they feel for us and how unfair it is. Many times I have asked, "Why did this happen to us?" (and believe me, I experience every emotion imaginable *each day*). Is this unfair? Death is a human condition that is perhaps unfair to all of us, yet none of us will escape. The truth is, many people live under the illusion that as long as we are good people, only good things will happen to us. And, if we eat right and exercise and do all the good stuff, we live as if we will never die. It is not really a question of fairness. I ask myself, how can all the blessings of a remarkably magical and full life I experienced with Richard leave me feeling like anything in my life has been unfair, including his early departure? The fact that I am not prone to feeling this kind of resentment in his loss is a testament to his love and the manner in which we navigated life together. It is a testament to the power of love and a life well-lived.

People ask me about my future a lot, and I say, what future? I have only to account for now. Staying in the present is the only way for me to live through this and not slip into the deep, dark hole that awaits all of us if we let it. I can only account for this moment and this day, as Richard has taught me by example that this is all any one of us really has.

In fact, the exception to this is when Richard jumped forward to look back. He questioned his mortality in order to live more fully in the present, as if each day was going to be his last. This is what his message to me on our anniversary is about. What a gift! My husband actually wrote me a letter in the event that he might suddenly walk out the door and not return. As it turns out, he has left this earth remarkably complete, and has given me such comfort and peace in the face of the dark night of the soul. What a profound example to his legacy; what an astounding teacher! Richard lived as an ordinary man willing to say extraordinary things and then, with the highest amount of integrity, live the principles he prescribed, to walk his talk with humility and grace. Whether it be his personal assistant, the grocery clerk, or the Dalai Lama, he treated everyone with the same gentle loving-kindness.

I learned so much from Richard in our lifetime together. Who knew I would learn just as much in his death? I have never known anything quite as effective as grief to break down the barriers of ego to open the spirit. I used to watch Richard speak, and see him reach far into himself and his divine state of being. His presence was so powerful. He didn't use a booming voice; rather more of a whisper. He was so quiet, and in his true nature, he was mesmerizing to watch. His audience barely breathed so they could hear his every word. It was magical because he exuded inner peace and authenticity, while everyone in the room felt his presence.

In the opening of my spirit from this loss, I have found meaning in carrying on the legacy of Richard's life and message. It is impossible for me to think of moving forward in this world in any other way. Life is a big experience and holds everything in it, and much of it we would not consciously choose—especially the suffering. Richard and I now meet in our spirits through divine consciousness. Our love as a conduit continues on, transcending the boundaries of time and space. While human separation is painful at best, I have discovered peace in knowing that great love is truly eternal and lives on forever.

This is a love story, but it also reveals a love affair with life. Our love is an example of what is possible in all relationships. Any one of us can take the time to notice and appreciate the gifts of any significant person, whether it is a spouse, parent, child, brother, sister, teacher, or friend. Why do we hold back what is in our hearts and take for granted those special people with whom we spend the most time? People want to know that they lived well, and loved well, and each of us has the power to share this gift. The most important question we can ask is: What kind of relationships do we want to have, and how can we nourish others so that we are nourished? Why wait to share the meaning of those relationships and withhold the gift of giving the most extraordinary kind of love—heartfelt appreciation? We can all leave this world as complete as Richard did by taking the time to reflect on the meaning of our most significant connections and how we can best serve. Why are you waiting?

Loving Richard and being loved by him with such an unconditional force truly healed me, and changed the course of my life as a human being. Even during our toughest times, dealing with the stresses of everyday life that everyone deals with, we handled issues with loving care of each other and our girls. We rarely took our low moods out on each other, and if we did, there was immediate apology and heartfelt connection to follow. Paramount to the strength of our connection was always the question, how can I help and support you? We had complete respect for each other, and while we knew we were a team, we also recognized our individuality. Our relationship was a rare thing in this world, and it was as if we were constantly tossing a ball, with ease, back and forth.

To be perfectly clear, all that Richard wrote to me in this letter would serve as a mirror reflection of all that he gave back to me and more. The truth is, I had to work hard to pull my own weight in our marriage and life together because Richard seemed to have boundless energy and never tired of serving. It always boggled my mind how he could have a more-than-full-time career, be completely devoted to his family, have lunch with his friends, attend all his daughters' soccer games and cheerleading competitions, and often bring dinner home by five p.m. The man was the calmest, most productive man alive. Even with the physical suffering he endured the last three years due to collapsed lower lumbar disks in his spine, he never complained or troubled those around him; he turned inward to his divine nature for comfort to write even more columns and books. He left this earth with little attachment to material things, but a great magnitude of appreciation for the love and connection that he cherished in his relationships. Richard Carlson walked among us and served as an example of a man with a pure heart who lived and loved with divine intention.

Each day I feel Richard. When I'm in my truest nature, I carry him in my heart; I can hear him like a whisper drowning out the noise of uncertainty and fear and loss. Marriage is the nexus of the physical and the spiritual; I have lost Richard in the physical sense, but our spiritual connection keeps on. Love does last forever. There is divine order. I believe even the smallest, most seemingly insignificant act of love continues on forever.

More about Richard Carlson can be found
on the following Web sites:

www.DontSweat.com

www.RichardCarlson.com (the memorial site)

Richard's favorite poem, by Norma Cornett Marek,
is reprinted below.

❧

Tomorrow Never Comes

If I knew it would be the last time that I'd see you
    fall asleep,
I would tuck you in more tightly, and pray the Lord
    your soul to keep.
If I knew it would be the last time that I'd see you
    walk out the door,
I would give you a hug and kiss, and call you back
    for just one more.

If I knew it would be the last time I'd hear your
    voice lifted up in praise,

I would tape each word and action, and play them
    back throughout my days.

If I knew it would be the last time, I would spare an
    extra minute or two,

To stop and say "I love you," instead of assuming
    you know I do.

So just in case tomorrow never comes, and today is
    all I get,

I'd like to say how much I love you, and I hope we
    never will forget.

Tomorrow is not promised to anyone, young or old
    alike,

And today may be the last chance you get to hold
   your loved one tight.

So if you're waiting for tomorrow, why not do it
   today?
For if tomorrow never comes, you'll surely regret
   the day
That you didn't take that extra time for a smile, a
   hug, or a kiss,
And you were too busy to grant someone, what
   turned out to be their one last wish.

So hold your loved ones close today, and whisper in
   their ear,
That you love them very much, and you'll always
   hold them dear.

Take time to say "I'm sorry," "Please forgive me,"
"thank you" or "it's okay."
And if tomorrow never comes, you'll have no
regrets about today.

—NORMA CORNETT MAREK

Tomorrow Never Comes *is dedicated*
in loving memory of Sammy,
son of Norma Cornett Marek.
Reprinted with permission.

ON THE FOLLOWING pages, write your own answers to the questions, "If you had one hour to live and could make just one phone call, who would it be to, what would you say, and why are you waiting?"

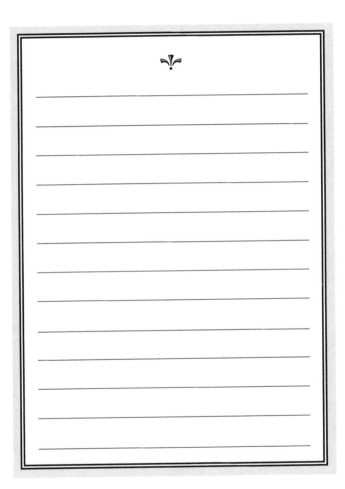

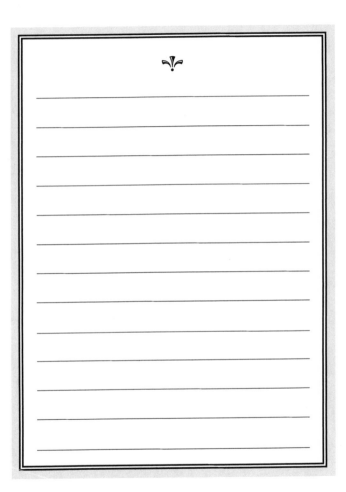

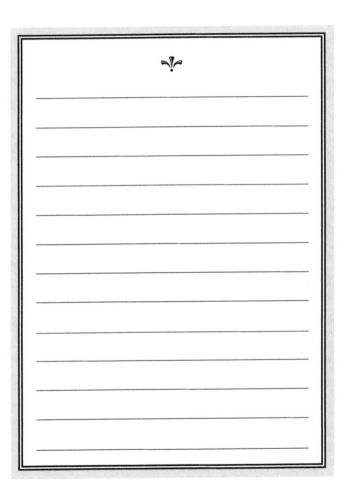